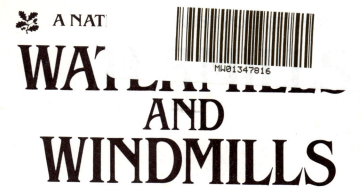

WATERMILLS AND WINDMILLS

By
J. KENNETH MAJOR

INTRODUCTION

The purpose of this handbook is to give the reader some knowledge of the construction of watermills and windmills together with a brief history of their development. The book then goes on to describe each of those mills belonging to the National Trust which can be visited, giving details of any outstanding features.

The use of natural forms of power, in this case water and wind, has always excited man's interest. The watermills of Britain together with the windmills show how man has adapted these forms of natural power to provide daily bread for himself and food for his animals. While the ubiquitous corn-mill remains uppermost in the minds of most visitors to watermills and windmills, it must be borne in mind that water-power was the initial source of energy which fuelled the growth of the Industrial Revolution in the early eighteenth century. So to corn-mills must be added cotton- and woollen-mills as users of water-power, and then the sawing of wood, the rolling of iron and the production of edge tools in both forges and grinding shops. All surviving windmills were built for the grinding of corn or the pumping of water, but at one time windmills provided power for a number of other industrial uses.

It is hoped that users of this handbook will gain greater enjoyment and understanding of windmills and watermills as they visit the countryside.

WATERMILLS

Corn is converted into meal by being ground between a rotating millstone and a fixed millstone. As the rotating millstone forces the grain between it and the bedstone, a tearing action reduces the grain to meal. The rotating millstone is powered by the natural force of water turning a water-wheel. The rotation of the water-wheel is transmitted to the millstones by means of the main shaft and first gearwheel, known as the 'pit wheel'. The pit wheel translates the horizontal rotation of the main shaft to the upright shaft. To do this it is engaged with the wallower, the first gearwheel on this shaft. Above the wallower there is the great spur-wheel, and that wheel has teeth round its circumference which engage with the smaller gearwheels which are on the spindles which rotate the upper, or runner, millstones. These smaller gearwheels are called 'stone nuts'.

The millstones, described as a 'pair' of millstones, consist of a lower fixed stone – called a 'bedstone' – and the upper (runner) stone which rotates. The faces between the stones are marked with a series of furrows and flat portions which together form the millstone dress. This dress is cut into the faces of the stone by the miller or by a millstone-dresser, using steel chisels called 'bills' which are mounted loosely in a wooden handle called a 'thrift'. So many bills are necessary in dressing a pair of millstones that they have to be changed frequently, and when the dressing is finished they all have to be resharpened. The action of the furrows is to cut the grain between their two upright walls, and the grain is reduced progressively as it goes from the edge of the stone to the circumference. To regulate the flow of meal, the millstones are enclosed in a casing, or tun,

A millstone dresser at work

which empties through a spout to sacks on the floor below. The casing supports a frame called a 'horse' which in turn supports the hopper and the shoe along which the grain passes to the eye of the rotating millstone. The shoe, on to which the grain drops from the hopper, is vibrated by the damozel. The damozel is an iron shaft with a claw which sits on the head of the stone spindle, and when it rotates its three or four arms vibrate the shoe.

The meal in the sacks below the millstones needs to be graded before it can be sold as flour. The sacks must, therefore, be taken back up through the mill to storage-bins at high level. The sacks pass up through the sack traps in the mill on the chain which is wound up by the sack hoist. The sack hoist and other machinery in the mill is powered by the extension of the upright shaft above the stone floor. The stone floor is the floor on which the millstones are mounted. The upright shaft carries a crown wheel near the ceiling of the stone floor, and this is a wheel which has its teeth facing upwards and with which other, smaller, gearwheels engage. These smaller wheels drive horizontal, or lay, shafts on which pulley wheels are mounted. The sack-hoist belt usually hangs loosely between the pulleys on the lay shaft and the sack-hoist shaft. To engage the hoist and get the sacks moving, the belt is tightened. The controls for the sack hoist will be in the form of toggles on a rope at each floor level in the mill. The rope is pulled and the sack-hoist shaft either moves up to tighten the drive belt, or the drive belt is moved over by means of a jockey pulley to create friction on the drive pulley and the sack-hoist pulley. The sacks come up through the sack traps which consist of two boards which are hinged so that the sack knocks them up and they fall back into place after its passage through them.

The meal passes through a wire brushing machine for its first grading. The wire brushing machine is a large box, with removable sides, which contains a cylinder of various grades of wire mesh mounted at an angle. Inside the cylinder a series of brushes are rotated so that the meal, as it goes down the wire cylinder, falls through the appropriately sized hole. Thus the meal is graded, leaving an unwanted grade, the 'tailing', to be used for animal fodder. If the meal requires further grading into

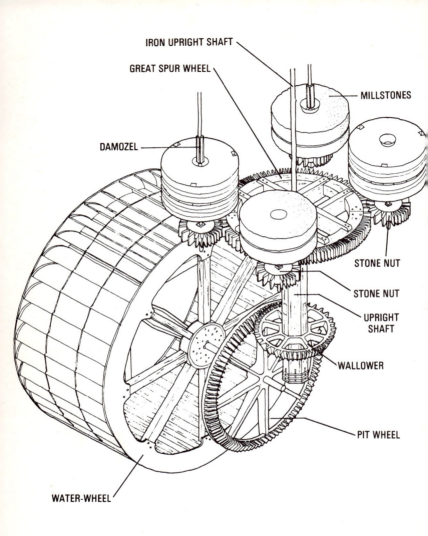

Typical watermill gearing

flour, it can be passed through a silk machine or bolter – a longer cylinder covered with various grades of silk mesh and set horizontally. Inside this machine wooden beaters force the meal through the appropriate sieve and this forms flour.

In practice the miller would receive the grain and hoist it to the storage floor at the top of the mill. It could be retained either in its original sacks or in bins. From there he would release it into the chute feeding the hopper on the millstones. He would then release the water on to the water-wheel by means of a hatch in the launder or mill-stream. He might have to close off the hatch which allows the water to escape when the water-wheel is not in use. The water-wheel would begin to turn and the miller would adjust the space between the millstones – 'tentering' is the word for this – to meet the speed of the water-wheel. He would judge the quality of the meal, rolling it between his thumb and forefinger, and get the adjustment right. While the mill would continue to work without his constant supervision, the miller would look to the tentering from time to time and keep the quality of the meal constant. He would also keep an eye on the smooth flow of grain into the hopper, and from the hopper to the shoe and then into the eye of the millstone. As the meal sacks were being filled on the floor below the stones, the miller would assemble them in readiness to pass them back up the mill, and from there the meal would go back through the dressing-machines to be collected in sacks at the lowest level. The finished products were often stored on the first floor (or stone floor) so that they could be moved on the sack barrow to the door at that level and slid down a chute on to the miller's cart. Early forms of automation were often present in nineteenth-century water-driven corn-mills and windmills enabling them to run for a long time unattended.

THE HISTORY OF WATERMILLS

The watermill which we know in Britain is one in which the water-wheel rotates in a vertical plane. It is known to have existed in Roman times for it is described by Vitruvius in his *De Architectura*, and is the basic design from which the present water-driven corn-mill derives. In Roman times the basic form consisted of a water-wheel fitted with blades or paddles, a toothed pinion fastened to the same shaft as the water-wheel, and a larger gearwheel mounted on a vertical spindle driving the millstone. In 1907 and 1908 F. Gerald Simpson excavated a Roman watermill at Haltwhistle Burn Head on the Roman Wall, and many other examples are known; indeed, a Roman water-driven water-raising device is preserved in the British Museum which assisted in mine drainage in the Rio Tinto Mines in Spain.

The vertical water-wheel is known to have been used in its various forms from earliest times. The simple classification is the overshot water-wheel, the breast-shot water-wheel and the undershot water-wheel. The overshot wheel is one in which the water is discharged from a launder into the buckets of the wheel at the top. The water in the buckets then carries the wheel in the same direction as the flow of water, that is, clockwise. This type of water-wheel must contain the water in buckets for the water remains in the wheel until it has all emptied out at the bottom. The breast-shot water-wheel is one in which the water comes from the mill-pond and strikes the wheel in the middle approximately on a line with the centre of the shaft. The water pushes the wheel round and the wheel rotates in the opposite direction to the flow of water, that is, anti-clockwise. The water is usually contained by flat or curved floats and by the curved sill round the wheel. The undershot water-wheel is driven by water striking the floats or paddles at the bottom of the wheel and driving it forward, that is, anti-clockwise.

In parallel with the development of the vertical water-wheel it is known that horizontal water-wheels came to be used in Britain. For example, in excavations of the Saxon strata of the town of Tamworth in Staffordshire, a watermill with two horizontal water-wheels was discovered. In these mills the millstones were driven directly by a water-wheel moving in a horizontal plane and mounted on the same spindle as the millstone which it drove. In Britain there is now only one preserved horizontal mill, that at Dounby on Orkney, although there must have been many in Orkney, Shetland and mainland Scotland in the past, where remains may still be found. The horizontal mill is the precursor of the first water turbines of the nineteenth century and the sophisticated turbines of the twentieth century.

The main stream of watermill design in Britain can be assumed to follow the Roman or Vitruvian form. In the Middle Ages this is clearly the case, and the corn-mill of that time will not have moved very far from that principle in which only one pair of millstones was driven by a water-wheel, with the gear on the main shaft engaging with a gear on the stone spindle. The speed at which the millstone turned would be greater than the speed of the water-wheel if a pair of gears which gave a

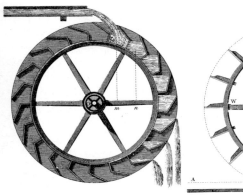

Overshot wheel

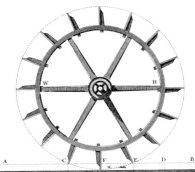

Stream wheel

Undershot wheel

Breastshot wheel

Types of water-wheel

10

step up in the speed were used. For a pair of stones 4 feet in diameter a rotation of 100 to 120 r.p.m. is necessary. If the water-wheel was rotating at 15 r.p.m., then the gear ratio would have to be 6 to 1 up to 8 to 1. In the medieval mill all the gearing and the water-wheel itself would be made of wood. The only iron would be the bearing pieces and the millstone spindles. Iron was expensive, and its use would be kept to a minimum.

Other industrial uses for water-power were initiated in the medieval period. For example, the great medieval architect Villard d'Honnecourt drew a water-driven up-and-down mechanical saw in the early part of the thirteenth century. It is known that water-wheels were used in mining practice for the crushing of ore, the raising of water by pumping and the raising of men and materials from the mines. Iron-working grew in volume during this period and water-driven forges came into operation; those in the Cistercian Kirkstall Abbey were in use by 1400.

As the medieval period gave way to the greater prosperity and learning of the post-Reformation period the use of machinery driven by water became more sophisticated. The publication in 1556 of Georgius Agricola's *De Re Metallica*, led to great improvements. The woodcuts in this book gave ideas and inspiration to mine-owners for improvements to their plant and equipment. The movement of mining engineers, masons and architects about Europe meant that ideas were quickly put into practice in the various countries at about the same time.

The use of the cog and rung type of gearing was all that was known until the eighteenth century. The great disadvantage of cog and rung gears is that they do not work smoothly but give a jerky, knocking motion. The introduction of the gear teeth which are seen in mills nowadays and by which a smooth rolling motion is achieved, took place in the middle of the eighteenth century. This introduction was the result of theories presented by the mathematicians of the time and the translation of those theories into practice by the millwright engineers. Up until the middle of the eighteenth century all the mill-work, as the gearing, shafts and mechanical systems are called, was made of wood with the minimum use of iron. At the beginning of the eighteenth century came the production of cheaper iron when coke replaced scarce and expensive charcoal in the smelting process. Gradually cast iron and wrought iron came into use in millwrighting practice.

The eighteenth century also saw the first attempts to apply scientific theories to the practical details of millwork. John Smeaton carried out experiments in the design of water-wheels and the sails of windmills. He took the designs he found in the great Dutch millwrighting textbooks of the 1730s and attempted to rationalise them. He analysed the various factors which govern the design of water-wheels and showed how the relationship between the volume of water available and the head of water at the wheel governed the choice of water-wheel for a particular mill. He published details of his experiments and after his death a number of his designs were published.

Smeaton, as a civil engineer, was followed by millwrights who also published their findings. Such a one was Andrew Gray, a Scotsman who, in 1803, published *The Experienced Millwright*, which contained general designs for many forms of mill; from animal-powered threshing-machines to large corn-mills powered by animals, wind or water. In the United States in 1795 Oliver Evans wrote and published *The Young Mill-wright and Miller's Guide* to assist country millwrights in the design of water-powered corn-mills. Because of the general shortage of labour in the United States, his mills incorporated a larger measure of automation than had formerly been obtained. He introduced the elevator, a continuous belt on which cups carry the grain and meal up through the mill, and Archimedean screws which carry the meal horizontally round the mill.

The ready availability of cast iron meant that water-wheels could be built to better designs and that they would, in fact, last longer. The water-wheel at Cotehele Mill (N.T.) is an interesting combination of iron shrouds with wooden spokes and wooden buckets. The introduction of iron made it possible to construct larger, and, therefore, more powerful wheels, and it was these wheels which powered the textile-mills which were built, like Quarry Bank Mill, Styal Village (N.T.), on the rivers running off the Pennines.

The growth in the use of water-power and the increasing mechanisation of the textile-mills meant that the millwrights ceased to be small rural craftsmen and became the owners of large factories. These factories, usually based in the North, produced not only an enormous number of water-wheels but also the millwork of complete mills. The water-wheels manufactured by firms like Hewes & Wren, Lillie & Fairbairn, and William Fairbairn became well known and their designs were copied by lesser firms. The original water-wheel at Styal was 32 feet in diameter and 24 feet wide

Houghton Mill. Gearing and millstones which are being driven from above

and was installed by Thomas Hewes in 1819. The new wheel being installed by the National Trust was designed and manufactured by William Fairbairn and comes from Glasshouses in Yorkshire. In country districts the iron mill-work was made by local foundries to the order of the millwright. One such foundry was Bodley's of Exeter who were in business from the late eighteenth century until the 1960s, and whose water-wheels were to be found over a very large area of the South-West.

The new designs of water-wheels, while coming into increasing use in textile-mills and other industrial plant, also had their impact on the design of corn-mills. The greater power of water-wheels enabled the miller either

to place a larger number of pairs of millstones in his watermill or to increase the number of water-wheels as at Houghton Mill in Cambridgeshire (N.T.). This increase in the production of the corn-mills matched the growth in population, particularly in the towns, and marked a change in the economy of the mill. In the Middle Ages the miller had been tied to his mill and his customers had been obliged to use the mill which stood on their landlord's manor, and his trade was governed by strict regulations. The return for the miller's work was governed by the milling soke. This meant that the miller received a quantity of grain from his customer which he turned into meal. He then returned the meal to the customer, but first taking out that portion – the multure – which was his due. The multure could be one-eighth, one-tenth, one-twelfth or one-sixteenth, according to the particular milling soke. This procedure prevailed long after the breakdown of the manorial system and the multure method existed as a means of payment at these 'toll' mills into the nineteenth century. With an increasing number of customers who were not producers of grain, the miller became a trader; buying grain in the market or direct from farmers and selling the meal, flour and animal feeds back to the bakers, farmers and wholesalers.

In 1829 the roller-mill was invented in Hungary and its introduction into Britain gathered momentum as the need to produce large amounts of flour brought increasing pressure on the miller. The country was ceasing to be self-sufficient in grain, and the American prairie farmers began their export of grain to Britain. The processing of the grain took place at the ports with Avonmouth, Tilbury, Gateshead-on-Tyne and Liverpool being among the earliest port mills. It was the growth of the port mills which spelt the economic end of the small water-powered corn-mill, such as those at Shalford, Bateman's and Nether Alderley.

Water-raising is an historic use of water-power which is as old as corn-milling. The fertile countries of the Middle East – Iraq, Iran and Egypt – are known to have had water-wheels which lifted water to a higher level in pots or scoops. The water-wheel would be driven round by the flow of a stream into which it dipped, the pots would fill as it dipped, and as they passed the top position of the wheel they would empty into runnels which carried the water to the land. The two great wheels at Hama in Syria are examples of this. While this form of wheel is still known in the Middle East, and there are examples in the north of Germany, none now exists in Britain. However, there is an extensive history of raising water for human consumption from the sixteenth century in some of our larger towns. In the Elizabethan Age water-wheels to supply Londoners with water were built in the northern arches of London Bridge. The water was stored in a tower and then delivered in pipes to conduit heads some distance away. At the end of the seventeenth century there were several waterworks established, again in our larger towns. Towns such as Doncaster, Leeds, Bridgnorth, Reading and Windsor had water-wheels, water-pumps and water-towers installed between 1690 and 1710. While the names of some of the water-engineers are known, George Sorocold of Derby is by far the most outstanding. With the increasing concern for wholesome water the owners of large houses established means whereby their water could be obtained from a pure source. Some owners, therefore, installed water-pumping devices driven by a water-wheel or by animal power, on their estates. Some of the mill-work which these water-wheel-driven pumps contain is of a high quality and represents considerable technical innovation. Dunham Massey (N.T.) has a water-wheel-driven pump on display, and these also exist at The Vyne, and at South Harting to supply Uppark with water. They contain small water-wheels coupled to cylinder pumps which pumped the water up to tanks at the top of the houses.

The watermill is an exciting part of our heritage and excellent examples of preserved mills can be seen in various parts of Britain. Those protected by the National Trust show the various forms of corn-mill, from the unsophisticated village mill to the highly skilled mill-work of the big mill, and also exhibit industrial uses such as cotton manufacture, linen production, wood-sawing, metal-refining and gunpowder manufacture.

WINDMILLS

The wind acting on the sails of a windmill drives them round and the power of this motion enables corn to be ground or water to be pumped. It is essential, therefore, that the sails are placed as high on the mill as possible so that they catch the full flow of the wind. A second prerequisite is that the wind always blows at right angles to the plane of the sails.

The windmills in Britain fall into three classifications: the post-mill, the tower mill and the smock-mill. The post-mill is a windmill in which the whole of the body of the mill is turned so that the sails face the wind. The tower mill is a tower of brick or stone in which the millstones and gearing are fixed and in which only the cap and sails are turned to face the wind. The smock-mill is similar to the tower mill, except that its body is a wooden structure clad with weatherboarding; its cap and sails are also turned to face the wind.

The post-mill is typified by Pitstone Windmill at Ivinghoe (N.T.). In a post-mill the body, or buck, is supported on a massive king-post which runs up to the beam under the first floor. The king-post is mounted above two horizontal timbers called the 'cross-trees' and is supported by the four quarter-bars. The cross-trees are supported above the ground on four brick piers. It is usual to find the supporting structure of the post-mill enclosed in a round-house of brick or stone with a slate

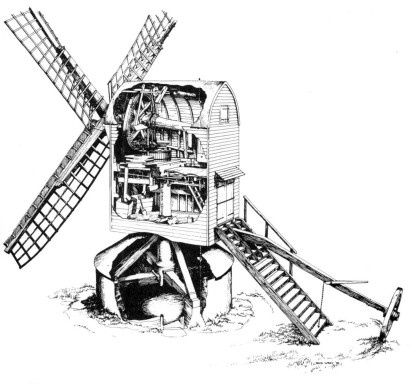

Pitstone Windmill – a post-mill. (Drawing by David Wray)

roof which goes up to the king-post under the body. This round-house provides protection for the vulnerable timbers and also provides additional storage for the mill as the body of a post-mill is usually very cramped because of the machinery and its size.

The body of the post-mill is made of a heavy timber

frame which is carried by the beams at first-floor level. The main beam which pivots on the king-post is the crown tree, and this carries the side girts on either side of the body. Above the first floor the framing of the body carries the beams which run parallel to the crown tree, and which carry the wind-shaft, sails and gearwheels. The main beam which carries the front, or neck-, bearing of the wind-shaft is called the 'weather-beam'. The beam at the other end is called the 'tail-beam' and this carries the tail-bearing of the wind-shaft. At the lowest level of the body two beams carry the floor and run on either side of the king-post at right angles to the crown tree. Between these the tail-pole is mounted and this extends down to the ground outside the rear of the mill. The body and roof of the post-mill are usually covered in weatherboarding.

The sails of a windmill are usually made up in two parts. The structure of a four-sailed mill consists of two sail stocks which are heavy timbers threaded through the sockets at the end of the wind-shaft. If these sockets and the neck bearing are made of cast iron they are called the 'canister'. The stocks extend equally on either side of the canister and usually reduce in thickness near their ends. On the sail stocks the sail whips are mounted and clamped. The whips are the main element of a sail which is formed up on these. The whip has the sail bars socketed through it at varying angles to give the 'weather' to the sails. On the sail bars are fixed the laths, and the outer ones are known as 'hemlaths'. At the inner end of the sail there is a rod on which rings are mounted just like a curtain-rail. This curtain-rail carries the sailcloth which is usually made of canvas. The variations in sail form will be dealt with later, but the canvas sail on the laths and sail bars is the original form of the sail and is known as the 'common sail'.

The wind-shaft in the post-mill carries a brake wheel inside the body of the mill. The brake wheel is equivalent to the pit wheel of the watermill. It is the first gearwheel taking the power of the sails down to the millstones. It is called the brake wheel because it is contained within a series of wooden brake-shoes or an iron brake-band which is clamped down by a lever to slow the mill, stop it, or prevent it starting. One danger in windmills is that the wind can strengthen and cause the sails to rotate which, if the mill is unattended, can turn the millstones and cause sparks and possibly fire. In the post-mill there would originally have been only one pair of millstones. Now there are often two pairs which can be sited either across the mill, as at Pitstone (N.T.), or one at the front and one at the back. If the millstones are set across the mill they are driven by an arrangement which resembles the watermill in reverse. In this the brake wheel engages with a wallower on an upright shaft which carries the great spur-wheel. The great spur-wheel, in turn, engages with the stone nuts which drive the runner stones of the pairs of millstones. When the two pairs of millstones are set with one at the front and one at the back, the brake wheel engages with the stone nut of the front pair of millstones and a similar tail wheel engages with the stone nut of the rear pair. In this case, of course, the millstones are driven from above – overdrift, as they are at Saxtead Green (D.O.E.). In the other arrangement the millstones can be driven from below – underdrift, as they are at Pitstone Windmill.

The millstones are the most important element of either a watermill or a windmill as they form the first

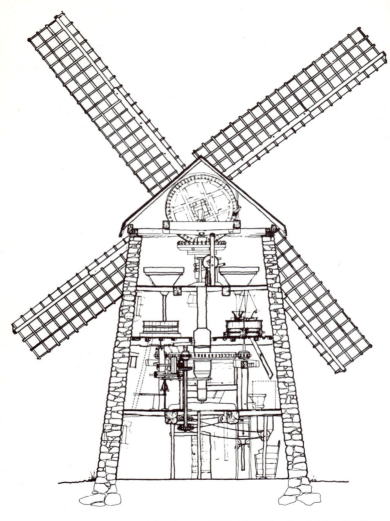

A cross section of Bembridge Tower Mill. (Drawing by Adrian Peel)

step in the reduction of grain to meal and flour. Millstones are made from various materials, but the two materials met with in mills today are Peak stone and French burr stone.

Peak stone, which comes from the Derbyshire Peak District, is a millstone grit. The Peak stone can be quarried in pieces large enough for a millstone to be cut out whole. The quarries for Peak stone can still be seen on Millstone Edge which stretches along the ridge to the east of the River Derwent in Derbyshire, from Matlock to Hathersage.

French burr stone is a stone imported from the quarries around La Ferté-sous-Jouarre in the Paris Basin. This stone is a freshwater quartz but it does not come out of the quarries in large pieces, so the millstones have to be built up by the pieces being bonded together, that is bound together with a steel band shrunk round the outside, and backed and jointed with plaster of Paris.

The stones have to be cut or made so that they hang level on the stone spindle. To do this properly and to ensure a level motion when they rotate, they have special boxes built into their backs – usually three – into which lead can be poured until they are properly balanced.

Other stone can be used for millstones. In the South-West and in Wales a conglomerate stone is used which forms a one-piece millstone. Some stones are a deep purple colour and have a texture like 'Aero' chocolate, and these come from the Eifel region of Germany. Because in medieval times they came down the Rhine by boat they became known as Cullin stones – Cullin being a corruption of Cologne. In recent times stones have been made of grains of emery, flint or burr stone bound with cementitious material, and these are known as composition stones. Peak stones and conglomerate stones are used to grind the grist (or animal feed), while French burr stones, Cullin stones and composition stones are used in the production of meal for flour.

The runner millstone is supported on the head of the stone spindle by means of the mace or the rind. The rind is the earlier form of support of the millstone, and consisted of a cross, + or ×, let into the underside of the runner millstone and sealed there by running hot lead round the four arms. The centre of the rind had a socket which fitted over the head of the stone spindle. The mace is the currently accepted method of carrying the runner stone. This consists of a heavy casting with a slot in the top and a socket for the head of the stone spindle on its underside. The millstone is carried on the mace by means of a bridge or a gimbal rind. The bridge is a bridge-shaped bar of iron; the two ends are leaded into the stone and the upward-facing bow sits in the slot on the mace. A gimbal rind is an oval shape of iron with two lugs on the outside which are leaded into the millstone and two lugs on the inside which sit in corresponding sockets in the mace. This form is difficult to balance but runs very true when it is properly balanced. The above describes the use of the stone spindle when it is driven from below the millstone. When the millstones are overdrift a spindle supports the runner stone from below and the stone spindle, or quant, which is driven from above the millstones fits over the mace to turn it and the millstones.

In the windmill, the arrangement by which the space between the millstones is adjusted is the same as it is in a watermill. The bearing at the base of the stone spindle is carried on a bridge-tree: a timber beam with one end hinged and the other adjusted by a screw. As the speed increases the millstones will go faster and the meal may become too fine and perhaps burnt by the overheating of the stones. The miller has to adjust the space between the stones to cope with the variations in speed. In a windmill, rather more than in a watermill, the speed variations can be quite extreme. One way of dealing with these variations is by the use of governors which will control the space between the millstones according to the speed of the wind. Rising-ball governors are usually set below the stone floor and are driven by pulley belts on the stone spindles. As the speed increases the rising balls raise the end of levers, or steelyards, and this in turn lowers the end of the bridge and lowers the runner stone so that it is closer to the bedstone. The presence of the grain and meal creates friction, and so if the sails are turning slowly then the opening between the millstones decreases the friction and the mill speeds up again.

The post-mill is turned to face the wind either manually or mechanically. To turn the mill manually the miller must first raise the foot of the mill ladder off the ground. If the post-mill is well balanced then he will be able to put his back to the tail-pole and push the mill round. At Pitstone the tail-pole has a cart-wheel on the end to support it. Sometimes the tail-pole is connected to a post set in the ground by a pulley system which winds the mill round when the miller pulls or winds in the rope. Mechanically, the mill can be turned automatically into the wind by means of a fantail. In this an annular-sailed wind-wheel stands out from the back of the mill and the end of the tail-ladder on a fan carriage. As the wind veers round so the wind-wheel begins to turn, and by means of gears turns wheels on the

The cap and winding gear of Bembridge Mill

fan carriage at the foot of the ladder. The ladder replaces the tail-pole in this arrangement.

Tower mills and smock-mills have similar gearing to each other which in turn has some similarity to the post-mill. As the mill body does not have to be pushed round, the tower mill or smock-mill can be much bigger and taller. Instead of two pairs of millstones, which is usual in post-mills, some tower mills and smock-mills have four pairs of millstones, all on one floor. The greater height of tower mills has the advantage of making the sails longer and, therefore, more powerful. The increased number of floors means that grain and meal can be stored above the stone floor and that dressing-machines can be properly sited to give their best service.

In a tower mill the cap will be carried on a curb on the top of the brick- or stonework, or in a smock-mill on top of the timber frame. The cap frame will have a heavy beam in the front to carry the neck-bearing of the sails, and towards the rear the tail-beam will carry the tail-bearing of the wind-shaft. The cap frame will extend out at the back to carry the fan carriage if the cap and sails are turned to the wind by a fantail, or the tail-pole and supporting struts if that method is used. The cap frame turns on the curb by means of rollers running in the cast-iron ring set at the top of the tower. This is called a 'live curb'; a dead curb is one in which the cap slides on the curb. To keep the cap properly centred there are wheels which run round the inside of the curb wall. The shape of the cap varies. In some areas the cap is boat shaped, in others semi-spherical, and in others it is ogee (S-shaped) in form. In some instances there is a gallery round the cap for maintenance of both the cap and body of the mill. Horsey Mill (N.T.) has a gallery round the cap, and this is typical of the wind-pumps of the Norfolk Broads.

The sails of tower mills do not always reach the ground so there is a reefing stage or balcony built round the mill, usually at first-floor level. This stage is particularly important in mills with common sails, for here the sailcloth has to be spread across the sail-frame or to be reefed to give a reduced sail area if the wind is strong. Certain types of shuttered sails also needed to be attended to from a reefing stage. In smock-mills the reefing stage is often built at the junction between the timber smock and its brick supporting base.

The gearing of the tower mill is very like that of the post-mill except that the increased height of the tower means that the upright shaft is longer. The brake wheel on the wind-shaft engages with the wallower at the head of the upright shaft. Sometimes a friction wheel attached to the sack-hoist windlass is raised by the sack-hoist control cord so that friction with the underside of the wallower lifts the sacks up the mill. The upright shaft can carry a crown wheel from which lay shafts extend to provide power from the ancillary machinery: the wire brushing machine and the silk machine, or bolter. The drive to the millstones can be overdrift or underdrift, and in the tower mill or smock-mill this is not dictated by the amount of space round the millstones but by regional preferences. Overdrift millstones predominate in the east and south-east of England and underdrift elsewhere. The great spur-wheels are, therefore, above or below the stone floor. The floors above the stone floor can be bin floors where the grain is stored prior to milling, and the floor immediately above the stone floor is used for the dressing-machines. The final product of meal, flour or animal feed is stored on the ground floor or the first floor, so that it can be more easily distributed or collected.

The use of windmills for drainage is thought to have been brought to England by the Dutch, particularly after the restoration of the Monarchy in 1660. The purpose of the drainage-mills is not to dry out land for reclamation but to regulate the level of the water around the reclaimed fields and in the soil to meet the needs of the farmers and the weather. In the Fens and Broads areas, where there was once an enormous number of windmills for drainage, the attendant of the drainage-mill was the employee of all the farms on that portion of land drained by a particular mill. There are two forms of water-raising device in drainage-mills which are still to be seen in England: these are the scoop-wheel and the turbine pump. The scoop-wheel is a wheel on which large radial paddles are set, and these paddles force the water from the lower level to the higher when the wheel rotates. The turbine pump, shown by Appold at the Great Exhibition of 1851, is more efficient and is completely contained within its housing. The drive from the sails is via gearing to the upright shaft which runs for the full height of the mill. At the foot bevel gears turn the motion at right angles into the shaft of the scoop-wheel, or to further gears on the top of the turbine pump.

The miller will ensure that he has hoisted all the grain required for a particular stint of grinding to the upper floor of his windmill. He will see to it that the grain is running smoothly into the hoppers and he will set the gap between the millstones wide. If he has common sails he will set the cloth on the lowest sail, then release the brake to bring the next sail to the bottom and set the cloth on that while it is held by the brake, and so on until all four cloths are set. Experience will tell the miller how much the sails should be reefed. He will then release the brake slowly so that the wind can give the sails momentum and the mill commence to grind. As the sails gain speed he will release the brake and close the gap between the stones. As in a watermill, he will watch the gap to ensure that the meal is of uniform quality. The meal will be bagged to be hoisted back up to the upper parts of the mill to be fed through the dressing-machines.

The miller working in a windmill has two great fears. First, that his mill will be back-winded, which means that the mill can be blown over if it is a post-mill, or its cap may be blown off in the case of a tower mill or smock-mill. The miller must watch the wind to ensure that, if it suddenly veers through 180 degrees as in a thunder squall, he can turn the mill. He watches the clouds for these can give him advance warning of coming storms. Second, he must ensure that the mill does not gain excessive speed if the wind rises in some unforeseen way. Excessive speed can cause fire at the brake wheel if it sparks or overheats with friction, and the overheating and sparking of the millstones can cause fire in the flour dust and softwood interior of the millstone casing.

THE HISTORY OF WINDMILLS

The use of the windmill in England is not so ancient as the use of the watermill. It is known that the first recorded windmills in England existed in the late twelfth century. The ancient manorial and monastic records show several examples of early windmills, and there have been several excavations of mounds in this country which have proved to be early windmill sites. At Great Linford in Milton Keynes, archaeologists have found an excellent example of a medieval post-mill. The dig revealed a cross in the ground filled with stones and timbers which was clearly the support of the cross-trees of a post-mill supported at ground-level; a quarter-bar was still jointed to a cross-tree. Post-mills often appear in medieval iconography: stained glass, illuminated manuscripts and church woodcarvings. Tower mills also existed but do not appear to have been so common and occur less in medieval iconography.

As with the watermill, the age of technological change in the windmill began about the middle of the eighteenth century with the innovation in gearing form and the introduction of cast iron. One important innovation was the fantail which enabled the miller to turn the mill or the cap into the wind. This is thought to be the invention of Edmund Lee in 1745 (Patent No. 615). The design of sails was investigated scientifically by John Smeaton in 1752–53. He had taken as his starting-point the empirical designs of the Dutch millwrights of the 1730s. In 1772 Andrew Meikle produced the spring sail. In this the shutters were pre-set from the tip of the sail to present the amount of opening that the wind speed required. As the wind rose or fell the pressure on the shutters opened or shut them against the control of the springs at the tip. In 1789 Captain Hooper invented a roller reefing sail which was controlled like the later 'patent' sail and which did not have the disadvantage of having to have the shutters set a sail at a time. The usual form of canvas-shuttered sail met with in England today is the 'patent' sail of Sir William Cubitt, which he patented in 1807. These shuttered sails are controlled by a rod which goes along each sail, connecting the shutters by bell cranks to the striking rod which goes through the centre of the wind-shaft to a rack at the rear of the mill. The gears on this rack engage with a pinion which is controlled by an endless chain with a weight at its lower end. The shutters can be adjusted without stopping the mill.

The windmill had begun its decline by the 1850s. It could not compete economically with the watermill which had greater capacity and was not so demanding of its miller and his staff. The introduction of roller-milling sealed its fate, and there are now only one or two windmills in England operating commercially.

NATIONAL TRUST WATERMILLS AND WINDMILLS OPEN TO THE PUBLIC

Buckinghamshire, Pitstone Windmill

Pitstone Windmill is a post-mill, with a round-house, which was built in the seventeenth century – a piece of the frame is dated 1627. The massive king-post on which the body of the mill rotates is original, and the body of the mill contains two pairs of millstones which are driven from below. The four cloth sails (common sails) are mounted on the wind-shaft and the drive is taken from this by the brake wheel and wallower. The mill was re-equipped in this manner in the nineteenth century. The mill was turned to face the wind by means of the tail-pole: the ladder was lifted, and the tail-pole supported on its cart-wheel was pushed round.

Pitstone Windmill is on the road from Ivinghoe to Tring (the B488) below Ivinghoe Beacon.

Cambridgeshire, Houghton Mill

This large watermill stands on the River Ouse and at one time barges could deliver grain to the mill where there is a lucam (a projection from the roof with a trap door in its floor) out over the upstream face. There were three large water-wheels, two on the south side and one on the north side, but these have all gone. Two of the three upright shafts are made of wood while the third is made of iron. Some gears are made of iron, others of wood and iron, with the oldest ones made entirely of wood. Note also that the drive to the millstones is quite different from the usual layout in mills. The gearing on the downstream shaft of the south side of the mill drove three pairs of millstones from a great spur-wheel above

Right: *Pitstone Windmill*

them, and a fourth pair of stones was driven from a horizontal shaft below the stone floor. The other water-wheel on the south side drove three pairs of stones in the conventional fashion, and the north water-wheel drove three pairs of stones from above. Houghton Mill represents the height of watermill design and was completed at a time when competitive roller-milling was starting in the ports. The iron mill-work shows the high point of engineering design as applied to the nineteenth-century watermill.

Houghton Mill stands just to the south of the centre of the village, to the south of the A1123, two and a half miles from St Ives.

Cambridgeshire, Lode Watermill, Anglesey Abbey

Lode Watermill lies at the head of Bottisham Lode and the mill-pond is, in fact, at the point where Quy Water discharges into the navigable lode in the village of Lode. The mill is three-storeyed with an attic, and clad with weatherboarding which is fixed vertically. The mill is a corn-mill with two pairs of millstones, but between 1900 and 1934 it was used to grind the materials for cement manufacture.

The water from the mill-pond drives the mill by means of an iron breast-shot water-wheel and by a conventional arrangement of pit wheel and wallower drives a wooden upright shaft. The two pairs of millstones are driven by the wooden great spur-wheel. The grain was raised to the top floor of the mill by means of the sack hoist. From the bins on the second floor the grain flowed down to the millstones, from whence the meal flowed to be bagged on the ground floor before

Left: *Houghton Mill, downstream view*

being taken back up by sack hoist to be dressed into flour. Note the big cast-iron signature plate in front of the upright shaft's bottom bearing; this has a magnificent quality and tells us that the mill was created in its present form by W. Rawlings in 1868.

Lode Watermill

Lode Watermill, the large signature plate

The mill is worked on occasion by the Cambridgeshire Wind and Watermill Society who repaired it between 1979 and 1982. The mill is reached through the Anglesey Abbey entrance and the beautiful formal gardens of the abbey which stand by the Cambridge to Mildenhall road, six miles north-east of Cambridge.

Cambridgeshire, Wicken Fen, The Wind-pump
This small drainage windmill built in 1908, was moved from the adjacent Adventurer's Fen in 1955 to pump water into the Wicken Fen Nature Reserve. It is a black weatherboarded smock-mill with four common sails and drives a scoop-wheel to lift the water, thus showing how the Fens were drained before steam, and then electricity, became available.

Wicken Fen Mill stands in the National Trust's Nature Reserve which is entered from the village of Wicken.

The wind-pump, Wicken Fen

Cheshire, Nether Alderley, Alderley Old Mill

References to a mill on this site can be traced back to 1391. It is one of the most fascinating of all English watermills. The walls are stone built and the building is roofed with the local stone slates. The rear of the mill nestles into the wall of the mill-dam so that there is only one storey projecting above the dam. The mill-pond is the moat of Alderley Old Hall. The mill roof rises one storey and then sweeps down through two storeys to be supported by a single-storey stone wall at the front. The arched remains of a drying-kiln stand at the end of the mill away from the water-wheels.

The height of the mill-dam makes it possible to have an unique arrangement of two water-wheels. The wheels are in the same plane and both are overshot. The water drives the upper wheel and discharges into a

Alderley Old Mill, Nether Alderley

channel from which it drives the lower wheel. The peculiar setting out of the two wheels has created an unusual disposition of the gearing and the millstones. The upper water-wheel drove two pairs of stones by means of an upright shaft but there is an additional short lay shaft between the water-wheel and the wallower. The lower water-wheel also drove two pairs of stones. At one time there were two mills separated by a wall across the full height of the present mill. Now it is possible to drive the stones from either wheel or both together, and this is an arrangement which dates from the time when the cast-iron hurst frame and gears were installed.

This watermill is by the A34, one and a half miles south of Alderley Edge and turns for demonstration and produces flour.

Cheshire, Styal Village, Quarry Bank Mill

In 1784 Samuel Greg founded the cotton-mill and industrial village which expanded in the nineteenth century to become the large complex which is now a working museum of the cotton industry of Lancashire and Cheshire.

From 1784 in various stages, culminating in the main alterations of 1836, the mill has grown into its present shape and size. The water-wheel, which is 32 feet in diameter and 24 feet wide, was built in 1819 by Thomas Hewes of Manchester in place of earlier wheels. This wheel was replaced by a turbine as the main source of power in 1903. Unfortunately the Hewes water-wheel was then broken up, but a wheel designed and manufactured by William Fairbairn has been installed subsequent to its removal from a textile-mill at

Glasshouses in Yorkshire. The power was taken from the water-wheel by a system of shafts and pulleys. This drove the spinning mules and looms, and power was later augmented by the addition of a steam engine.

The complex of the Quarry Bank site contains the apprentice house where the poor apprentices lived who had been brought from city workhouses. At Styal at the end of the eighteenth century Samuel Greg carried out many acts of welfare to improve the lot of his working people. He built the houses in Styal Village for his senior workers and to these he added a shop, allotments, gardens, a chapel and a schoolroom. In the factory area there are stables, a gasworks, warehouses and the manager's house, all of which show a high level of industry.

The water-wheel will eventually drive the machinery which is at present turning out cloth for sale. The machines can be seen working. The mill and village are eleven miles south-east of Manchester on the B5166.

Cornwall, Cotehele
The ancient estate of Cotehele contains an eighteenth-century water-driven corn-mill, a saw-mill, and wheelwright's and blacksmith's shops. Of great importance, too, is the Quay for the River Tamar was the highway for trade in this very hilly part of Cornwall. The sailing-barge *Shamrock*, which has been restored to its 1920s condition, is moored at the Quay. It is a barge similar to those built at Cotehele which carried produce down the river to Plymouth and Devonport.

The corn-mill is now powered by a large overshot water-wheel, but previously there was a second water-wheel behind this. There are three pairs of millstones

Cotehele Mill

and the associated dressing-machines. There is also a low-powered generator worked by the water-wheel. The fine mill building also contains an important example of a horse-engine. In this engine a horse walked round in a circle beneath a large gearwheel. As this gearwheel turned it engaged with gearing on an apple-crusher. The crushed apples were collected and placed in the massive cider-press, from which the juices ran to be made into cider.

This mill, which is worked on occasion, is eight miles south-west of Tavistock and can be reached by minor roads which lead off the A390. It is also possible to get to the mill by water using the service provided by the Millbrook Steamboat Company of Plymouth.

Cumbria, Sedgwick Gunpowder-mills

An important use of water-power in the Lake District was to drive the many machines and mills in a powder-works. Here at Sedgwick, as in the rest of Cumbria, the powder-mills made blasting powder for mining and quarrying and not for guns. This site, which is now a caravan park, is open to visitors who can explore the remains of the industry spread out along the waterways and leats over nearly half a mile on the west bank of the River Kent. Safety dictated the layout of the buildings so that when accidents happened the minimum of damage was caused to the works as a whole, and here one can see the buildings lying between protective banks and separated by quite some distance.

The water-wheels were used to drive the great edge-runner mills which crushed the charcoal, saltpetre and

An early drawing of Sedgwick Gunpowder-mills

sulphur and mixed them together. The powder was then pressed into slabs by screw presses or hydraulic presses. The resultant cake was broken up and graded into the various sizes of grain for the various kinds of job. The process ended with the powder being dried and then pressed into blasting cartridges into which a fuse was fitted.

Another element of the mill was the cooper's workshop for the powder was packed in barrels which protected it from weather and damage. A feature of the works was the railway system which connected one mill with another and carried wooden trucks on bronze wheels drawn by horses shod with bronze to prevent sparks.

The site is interesting, but whilst one can see the remains of blast walls, water-wheel pits and leats, there are no principal buildings in place. When a gunpowder works is shut down at the end of its life, the buildings have to be razed to prevent fires or explosions because the walls are covered with the remains of the gunpowder.

The gunpowder-mills can be reached from the roundabout at the junction of the A6 and A65, four miles south of Kendal.

East Sussex, Burwash, Park Mill, Bateman's

When Rudyard Kipling bought Bateman's he also bought the Park Mill on the estate. The present mill dates from about 1750 and it worked until 1902 when Rudyard Kipling took possession. Kipling removed the water-wheel and installed a turbine with which he produced his own electricity. The vortex turbine is an inward-flow turbine supplied by Gilbert Gilkes & Co. of

Park Mill, Bateman's, from the mill pond

Kendal in 1903. It generated some 4 h.p. and ran at 280 r.p.m. with an overall head of 12 feet. The direct current of 110 volts was produced on a Crompton & Co. generator.

The new water-wheel drove three pairs of millstones and the one enclosed in its casing is now producing meal from the grain. The others are open to demonstrate the dressing of the millstones with the tools: the thrift carrying the loose chisels – the mill bills. The gears turning the upper, or runner, stone are quite conventional: the pit wheel on the main shaft engaging with the wallower on the vertical shaft, and the great spur-wheel under the stone floor engaging with the stone nuts on the stone spindles. The vertical shaft goes up to drive the crown wheel which in turn drove the ancillary machines: the wire dressing machine, the smutter for cleaning grain and the sack hoist.

Bateman's lies half a mile south of Burwash on the A265 Hawkhurst to Heathfield road. The mill works and flour is produced for sale.

Essex, Colchester, Bourne Mill

This charming two-storey watermill with Dutch gables was built in 1591 as a corn-mill from the remains of a

Bourne Mill, Colchester, the downstream side

nearby abbey. During the Cromwellian period it was used as a cloth-mill and again became a corn-mill in the mid nineteenth century. The large overshot water-wheel is contained within the building and there is good wooden gearing which drove the three pairs of millstones. The mill-pond is a good place for waterfowl.

This watermill is in Bourne Road, off the B1025, one mile south of the centre of Colchester.

Greater Manchester, formerly Cheshire, Dunham Massey Saw-mill and Pump-house

In 1860 the corn-mill attached to the Dunham Massey estate was gutted and converted to the estate saw-mill. This saw-mill has now been restored to working order and machinery typical of the late nineteenth century has been installed. The overshot water-wheel, 15 feet 4 inches in diameter, and 3 feet wide, carries a small edge gearwheel on its main shaft and this in turn engages with a second gearwheel mounted on the same shaft as a large wooden pulley wheel. Belting from this pulley wheel drives a horizontal shaft, and at the opposite end of this shaft two belts driving an intermediate shaft set in motion a final shaft. This last shaft carries an iron flywheel which imparts an even motion to the saw and has a crank at its end which gives the saw its up-and-down motion. As the saw goes up and down in the saw-cut the log is propelled forward on its trolley by a ratchet device pushed along by a small crank at the opposite end of the final shaft. The other machinery which can be seen in addition to the up-and-down, or frame-, saw, is a circular-saw, a heavy-duty boring machine, a crane to lift the trunks on to the saw, a lathe which has a bed to accept work up to 10 feet in length, and a bandsaw of

1870. With the water-wheel producing about 10 h.p. it could probably work only one machine at a time.

Many large houses had water-wheel-driven pumps to supply their water and Dunham Massey is no exception. The brick building near the Orangery is the Pumphouse. The water-wheel was installed about 1860 and worked until about 1890 when it was replaced by an engine. The water-wheel drove a horizontal pump by a crank on its shaft with, adjacent to it, an air vessel to equalise the flow.

Dunham Massey is three miles south-west of Altrincham off the A56.

City Mill, Winchester

Hampshire, Winchester, City Mill

The River Itchen flows in many different watercourses as it passes through Winchester, and at one time powered a total of eleven water-driven corn-mills. The City Mill, near the centre of the city, dates from the reign of Richard Coeur-de-Lion, having been built by one of the many monasteries in the city. It has a continuous history of working until this century, when it came into the ownership of the National Trust who now lease it as a Youth Hostel. The mill in its present form was built in 1744 and consists of two storeys with a grain-storage attic. It is built of brick with tile-hung gables, and there is no gearing in place.

City Mill is at the foot of the High Street near the centre of Winchester.

Isle of Wight, Bembridge Windmill

This four-storeyed stone tower mill is dated 1746 and is representative of the mills of that period although its gearing has been renewed since then. There are four common sails and these are turned into the wind by means of an endless chain and wheel at the rear of the cap. There are two pairs of millstones and several dressing-machines on the first and ground floors. The gearing is of particular interest and the method of controlling the space between the millstones by means of governors connected to the bridge carrying the millstones is unique. There are several models and drawings of other mills on display.

This windmill stands near the road from Bembridge to Brading, the B3395.

Right: *Bembridge Windmill*

Norfolk, Burnham Market, Burnham Overy Mill

Burnham Overy watermill, together with the windmill close by, forms part of a large grain milling and processing complex near Burnham Overy Staithe. The brick-built tower mill is typical of Norfolk's wind-driven corn-mills, but it is not open to the public. The brick-built watermill is two storeys high with grain storage space in the attic. The grain enters the storage-space by being drawn up through the white-painted lucam on the main front. In the building on the west side of the mill, barley was turned into malt for brewery purposes. Barley is moistened and laid out on the malting floor to germinate. When germination has commenced the malt is heated in the malt-kiln to arrest the process before the grains are dispatched to the brewery. The characteristic louvred windows mark the germinating floors. Other buildings in the complex are barns, the miller's house and housing for mill employees.

Burnham Overy Mill is half a mile north-west of Burnham Overy Staithe on the A149 New Hunstanton to Wells road.

Norfolk, Horsey Drainage-windmill

Horsey Mill was rebuilt on an older site in 1912 by Dan England, a millwright famous for his work on the pumping-mills of Norfolk and Suffolk. The double-shuttered sails are mounted on a wooden boat-shaped cap with a fantail at the rear. The upright shaft descends to ground-level and bevel gears turned the drive into the pump-house beside the mill. Here a turbine pump lifted the water from the marsh to Horsey Mere.

This windmill stands by the road from Happisburgh to West Somerton (the B1159) just south of Horsey.

Left: *Burnham Overy Windmill*

Horsey Drainage-windmill

Somerset, Dunster Watermill

Dunster Watermill is a manorial mill serving both castle and village and may date from the seventeenth century. In its present form the mill dates from 1779–82. Two overshot water-wheels drive the mill and make a very attractive scene. The millstones are driven in the conventional way and the ancillary machinery remains in place in this two-storey stone mill.

This is a working watermill and visitors can buy its wholemeal flour. It is in Mill Lane in Dunster village, two miles south-east of Minehead on the A396.

Dunster Watermill

Somerset, High Ham, Stembridge Tower Mill

This tower mill is the only windmill in England which still retains a thatched cap. The mill stands on the low hills above the Somerset Levels, and this mill and the nearby tower mill at Chapel Allerton, are all that remain of a landscape which was once dotted with many windmills. The short stubby limestone tower contains two pairs of millstones: a pair of French burr stones and one pair made of sandstone conglomerate. The cap carries the wind-shaft and the sails are bolted to a cast-iron cross without any stocks. The sails were set from the circular mound which serves as a reefing stage. The wind-shaft carries a wooden brake wheel but the

Stembridge Tower Mill, High Ham

remainder of the gear and the millstone furniture is missing. As with many other windmills on exposed sites in the West Country there is a fireplace at ground-floor level which had an outlet just below the cap.

Stembridge Mill is two miles north of Langport on the A372.

Suffolk, Flatford Mill
Flatford Mill was the home of Golding Constable, the father of John Constable, until the family moved to East

Flatford Mill

Bergholt where John was born in 1776. The mill, which is the brick building facing the mill-pool and Willy Lott's cottage, has two arches in this face. The waterwheel, which was removed in 1901, stood at the back of the mill building in an extension over the mill-race. There is no machinery in the mill which is now used as a Field Study Centre.

While Flatford Mill cannot be entered by casual visitors, they can enjoy the site and gaze on the landscape so faithfully studied by John Constable. Flatford Mill is on the north bank of the River Stour, one mile south of East Bergholt.

Surrey, Shalford Mill
The River Tillingbourne flows under the middle of the mill at a point where the second floor extends out over

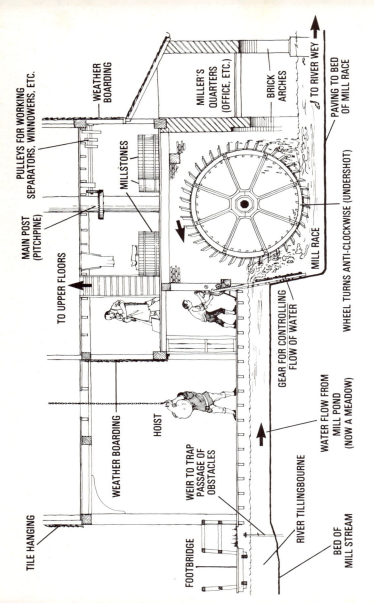

Shalford Watermill. (*Drawing by Brian Bagnall*)

Shalford Mill, the great spur wheel and wallower

the bridge to protect the miller's carts. The tile hanging and weatherboarding make this a picturesque mill set in a fine valley. The existing water-wheel and wooden gearing powered three pairs of millstones – two pairs of Peak stones and one pair of French burr stones on the first floor. The wooden upright shaft goes through the second floor to power two wire brushing machines, an oat-crusher and the drive to the sack hoist in the attic space.

The mill is situated down a little lane on the east side of the Guildford to Horsham road (the A281), one and a half miles from Guildford.

Northern Ireland, County Down, Castle Ward

Many big houses and estates had their own completely self-sufficient arrangements. Castle Ward is such a house and estate and in the lower farmyard there is an interesting complex of saw-mill, corn-mill and slaughterhouse as well as other buildings. The ornamental lakes were the power source for the water-driven saw-mill and corn-mill, and the water was also used to flush out the slaughterhouse. The low breast-shot water-wheel of the corn-mill, 13 feet in diameter and 5 feet wide, drove millstones for both the production of flour and animal feed. The saw-mill is worked for demonstration purposes and the slaughterhouse is open as an information centre.

The Castle Ward house and estate is seven miles north-east of Downpatrick off the A25 Downpatrick to Strangford road.

Northern Ireland, County Tyrone, Wellbrook Beetling-mill

Wellbrook Beetling-mill represents one use of water-power unknown in England and Wales. A beetling-mill is a mill in which a smooth glossy surface is formed on woven linen cloth to give it a sheen. Here the large breast-shot water-wheel, 16 feet in diameter and 4 feet 6 inches wide, powered a horizontal shaft which in turn drove the seven beetling-engines. In a beetling-engine the linen cloth was wound round a smooth wooden cylinder to be beaten by wooden hammers known as 'beetles'. Above the cylinder is mounted the wiper beam on to which thirty-two beech lifts are bolted. As the wiper beam is turned by the gearing on the shaft the thirty-two beetles rise and fall on to the cloth on the first cylinder which is also turning. The amount of beetling varied with the type of finish required, and when the cloth was taken off after two or three days it was hung in

Wellbrook Beetling-mill

the upper storey of the mill which was the drying-loft. The cloth was processed in bolts 23 yards long and was folded for dispatch in the loft.

Wellbrook Bettling-mill now houses a display of the history of the Northern Ireland linen industry as well as the original machinery of the beetling-mill. The water-wheel works, and beetling is demonstrated when the mill is open. The mill is two and a half miles west of Cookstown, just north of the B159 Cookstown to Omagh road.

Scotland, West Lothian, Preston Watermill
This fine watermill was built in 1660 as the local estate mill preparing oatmeal, wholemeal flour and animal

Preston Watermill

feed. At the north end of the watermill, linked by a bridge at first-floor level, is the circular drying-kiln. This kiln was where the grain, particularly oatmeal, was dried on a perforated floor over a peat or anthracite fire. A kiln which is circular is earlier in date than the square form usually to be met with in the North of England and in Scotland. The watermill is two-storeyed with the drive from the breast-shot water-wheel occupying the ground floor and the two pairs of millstones on the upper floor. The grain was taken to the millstones by the existing elevator and screw conveyor, but originally it would have been emptied sack by sack into hoppers over the millstones.

Preston Mill belongs to the National Trust for Scotland and stands by the B1407, half a mile north-east of East Lothian.

Wales, West Glamorgan, Aberdulais Falls
Aberdulais Falls is one of the most exciting of industrial sites. In 1584 a German mining engineer, Ulrich Frosse, set up a copper-smelting works at Aberdulais using the water-power created by the natural falls on this tributary of the River Neath, the Afon Dulais, almost at the confluence of the two rivers. At the present time one can see the foundations of many of the buildings, the pits which housed the many water-wheels, the chimneys and smelting sites. Later on corn-mills made use of the readily available water-power. As the smelting of copper moved to Swansea to take advantage of the harbour facilities, the work carried out on the site changed to tinplate-making and iron-rolling.

There is a good interpretative centre on the site. In this display the site and its surroundings are fully detailed so that one can see the history of the industries, the canals, the roads and the water-power. Several copies of famous paintings of the site help the interpretation.

The Falls are situated three miles north of Neath on the Neath to Merthyr Tydfil road.

Aberdulais Falls, a drawing of 1812